ATLAS OF ROOTS

01 02 03 04 05 25 24 23 22 21

Caitlin Press Inc.
8100 Alderwood Road,
Halfmoon Bay, BC V0N 1Y1
www.caitlin-press.com

Text and cover design by Vici Johnstone
Cover art by Andy Saputo
Printed in Canada

Caitlin Press Inc. acknowledges financial support from the Government of Canada and the Canada Council for the Arts, and the Province of British Columbia through the British Columbia Arts Council and the Book Publisher's Tax Credit.

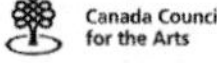

Library and Archives Canada Cataloguing in Publication

Atlas of roots / Beth Kope.
Kope, Beth, 1959– author.

Poems.
Canadiana 20200375296 | ISBN 9781773860510 (softcover)

LCC PS8621.O68 A75 2021 | DDC C811/.6—dc23

ATLAS OF ROOTS

Poems

Beth Kope

CAITLIN PRESS 2021

Story, for me, is a thing to revel in,

even when it ends in sadness.

Even when it's made of your own pain.

—Anita Lahey

To those who call me family, much love

Contents

I Origin/Original/Originate/

II To Search, Ransack Boxes

III Could One of These Stories Be Mine?

I

Origin/Original/Originate/

I Write Fictional History

to fill in the blank lines drawn on my skin
across my forehead and around my wrist like a band
of copper wire, tensile, drawn out.

I write history that is fiction

and interview everyone sideways. I talk
and they talk and I try to finish their sentences
and then I stop. Because that is rude.

I write what's spoken

then I write it again on a second page. I dream
of government forms that arrive in the mail. And
I read them out loud.

I write my future and present

but mainly my past, making it up as I go along.
There's the grandfather, the grandmother,
the villages their grandparents left and

I think of the chorus of stones
that sing in my blood, stories written
in lower Edwardian script on my genes.

I write history.

Enough to fill a book, fill
pages with facts
all made up.

I am child of

I come from

How to Pronounce Me

I entered the world
headfirst, my name embossed
in the white vernix
stretched across my back.

My name waited for me to claim it
but hands towelled and swaddled me
that name was wiped
onto hospital linens and washed away.

I have never loved my given name.
It feels wrong. I hate saying it.
I can't change it.
This burnt mouth name won't let me go.

Her first name.
His first name.
My real name.

I cannot properly be summoned.
Call me with your eyes not your mouth.

Conjure me.
I still wait for my name.

So-called

"Names have the power to summon. All witches and poets know this."
—Ana Maria Guay

You were named for your nana from Iceland.
        The men on the boat loved her,
        braids waist long, thick as her arm.

You were named for a girl I loved in grade two.

You were named after flowers in a cottage garden.

Your name was so popular, there were three in your class.

Your name came from God, He told us.

You were named for your birth
month, your birth day, your birth gemstone,

for the sound you made in the night.

How Does a Baby Come to Be?

You, baby, were brought to us by three crows. One
carried you, one carried your blanket, the other carried your name.

Fairies dropped you in the basket at our garden gate
where we usually find berries.

Floating on a lily pad.

There you were, playing with kittens in the pet shop window.

We dreamt you.

Your mother couldn't take care of you.
    She loved you so much, but she couldn't take care of you.
    She wanted you to have
    us. We wanted you.

sold, bought, traded, given, gifted, borrowed, owned, passed off

Different. But Better

This is the first story you're told. You were
chosen, from beginning, it's your story.
You are special and wanted.
Different, but better.

There are picture books to explain, where
the baby is white and eyes are blue
like the mommy and daddy
who took you home.

Your mother knew
when she saw you.
You were chosen.
And special. And wanted.

You're adopted. It's different.
For someone to choose you,
you were "given up"
by a birth mother and father, unformed
shadows at your shoulder.

Why Look for a Mother?

My mother left me. Mom left my side, disappeared
I was five, looked up:
        don't remember

        if she found me
        if she announced over loudspeakers
        if I was crying
        if I found her two aisles over
        if she grumbled at me to pay attention
        if she noticed

Which mother left me?

Cold

Search to find comfort, then, child.
Follow a forest path

salvage a nest, meager and mossy
torn from a branch in high winds.

Tuck the shredded remnant
into your pocket.

Hold to your quest.
To a distant mother

knowing some comforts are cold.

Chorus

"...we are like stones; our own history and the history of the world embedded in us, we hold a sorrow deep within...."
—Susan Griffin, *A Chorus of Stones*

I am stone holding secret, found in mud. I am the stone under water
scoured smooth. I am the stone tossed from your palm, a random
connect disconnect: what drew you to my shape, why did you lift me
from the beach?

I am the stone set on a windowsill for colour, for a heart shape. I am
the stone midway in the tower, a capstone, holding, stone force. I am
the stone that balances all. I am the stone you've dug up, tossed
to the pile along the fence.

I am the stone you hold in your pocket, absently caressed.

Lois Speaks to Her Three Children (I Answer Back)

To me:
I called your Nana and she came and showed me
how to bottle feed you, and your aunt gave you your first bath.
I was too scared your brown eyes, big, so big, looking up at me
and you cried and cried and cried such a colicky baby
To my sister:
Your dad and I
knew from the first time I saw
you were so tiny and underfed
your blue eyes
you grew in my heart not under
giving love is more than giving birth

To my brother:
You were chosen

To my sister:
you were chosen

To me:
you were chosen.

I Answer Back

There wasn't a row of babies in cots.
You didn't consider each one
until something stopped you.
pulled you close.
Choosing is what happens
when you find a litter of puppies.

Yours, not Yours

You are eight, maybe nine, another dinner with uncles, aunts,
Gran and cousins stitched around the dining room table and the talk
opens a window on family and past family all those names, stories
of farming and dust, Winnipeg and Hamiota, snow in winter,
dugouts, train trips into the city, orchards and horses, the family dog.

You are a kid and those uncles and aunts repeat those stories
that decode Helen's laugh, Charlie's love of opera, your father's
height, Anna Lopkin, great-great grandmother and how your cousin
is her spitting image. You are not.

You're puzzling out. Adopted great-great isn't your great-great and
if that great-great is not yours, then what of your mother father sister
brother the cousins and aunts and uncles, the Nana and the grandpa?
Yours. Not yours.

Blanks

I have one page, yellowed, folded, one paper
that spreads what I know of myself
thinly across it, letters drop from the edge
blow off the page from my sighs.

A smudge that may be the first letter
of my name has spilled off,
effaced, erased, unrecorded.

Connect/Connection

Who said the stars in the sky
connect to the moment of our birth?
Who believes those distant burning monsters
know our names, our ways of being?
Such superb faith in cosmic
filaments and fate.

Take a pencil. Connect numbered
dots in the workbook.
Lines complete a shape.
Then answer the question at the top of the page:

what does the child hold in her hands?
And colour the star yellow.

Here Is a Story of Our Growing Up

Imagine two sisters.
One is blonde, gorgeous, shy and soft-spoken.
The second is shorter, rounder, messier and loud
not as smart as she thinks, scared of her
moods, shelters in books.

You meet these two sisters. And of course, you say
"you two don't look alike."
And the dark, messy, sister spills out
"well that's because we are adopted."
Every time, it spills from her

and every time,
the tall blonde lovely sister
flees, under a blanket
shame of it all.

Silence (Another Part)

It was the silence

of questions that circle the house, sniff at the door, paw
against glass

of the pause as a blue vase tilts from the table edge
before shattering
of ice on a lake. Then add
the air above it.

Hand Me Down

The tremor in my hand is a constant reminder
of the shaky woman who raised me, her hand: open, close, caress
beat down.

I walk on early spring's unstable frost-heaves, sidewalk fissures:
stumble on what should be solid. The tremor in my hand is constant
the source is unknown.

What is cause? Effect? The tremor
in my hand is a constant variable.

Beyond paper, uncertain whose handwriting. Beyond
guess work or visual cues.
Whose words fray the page?

Grassland

I grew up in lands of grass. Where grass is more than lawn,
where grass bends to wind, waits to be plaited by breezes and gusts.
Where grass is fescue, sedge, feathery blue tips of and high, higher
than a toddler's stretch, an ocean of yellow and golden.
I grew up in grassland horizons, unbroken sweep of sighs.
Where roads run to the border of land and sky. Where land
stretches to edges, vacant, until hawk swoop, gopher dash,
snake's undulant shift to burrow.
I grew up where grass bent to birds, bore the tidy clutch
of a vesper sparrow.
Grass grew and there was always wind. Wind cradling a hush
of grass, a message of listening. A land of wind sheering bluffs
and glacial sculpting, of coyote lope and badger burrow,
of trembling aspen in deep coulees.

along the fence line, the worn path

so close, your leg whispers past wire.
There's the scraggy hill, a hollow and a copse of aspen
where dead centre, an old oil drum has rusted to orange lace.

You'll find the horses there, necks low, eyes
flickering at your steady approach.
Shadows lengthen out in late
afternoon.

You are home,
the halter in your hand
stiff and unbending
as you notch it round a scruffed neck.

It's summer, the horses' backs
flick with fly twitch.

It's cold and you break ice in the trough
thick enough to resist the horses' efforts.

It's any season, any day, any hour, moment
of home smells and lingering.

You know it well.

Where Do We Come From?

Once it was the spark from god's fingertip
and scooped grey-dark clay; we were
the very compost of Earth,
the loams and lone-ness
our parts and bones.

Once, we were the tip
of a branch of a tree, tenuous hold
on a blown branch, our opposable
thumbs barely hanging on, tossed
between mercies of wind and turbulent boughs.

Ask again: we come from where?

We were from demons spawned
by anger. We were from raven's mouth.
We were licked from the ice, sprung
from egg, avalanche of biology,
a salty bath.

Map It

Is my answer written
in blue ink
on a paper,
folded, slipped
in a sock drawer?

Unfold me now:

II

To Search, Ransack Boxes

Last Name

At the government adoption records office
for the province in Edmonton, Alberta
the man gives me
        a form to request more information
        a form to request contact
        a form to find relatives
        a form to request further medical information
        and the social worker's report.

He leans over and spells out this unfamiliar name, "for my search"
because I've misspelt it, and it sits on my tongue like lead. A lead.

Father Redacted

I can only imagine my father.
So few clues, no name. Only
The father is a moon-faced man.

There's nothing on his eyes
or height or hair
I only have

a current pulling me from shore, a riptide that won't release.
This strange phrase on my adoption form.
The father is a moon-faced man.

It grips me.
I ask for more, ask my mother
does moon-face mean an illness or disease?

Was he odd or slow?
Was it my birth mother's description of this man?
The social worker's choice?

I hunt for my adoption papers years later and
find they've disappeared, yet
certain I read that sentence

The father is a moon-faced man.

Lois Speaks to the Mothers of Her Children

1.
Yes, I took her from you.
This is the way a family
is built, the family I'm owed.
I was owed these children.
Owed now own.
This is the way a family should be:
two sisters and
a baby boy for good measure.
The father. The mother.
The family I'm owed, the three
who give me the mother hood I wear.

2.
I want to thank you. He
is the child of my heart
and will always be.
I want to thank you,
but you are too far away.

3.
You are in the corner of the bedroom again
watching me rock our baby
wailing. I rock her better than, sing
lullabies my own Nana gave,
bestow these songs, nestling,
but as she wails, I wonder
am I best for her, know you long
to sing your own songs.

My Sister's Birth Mother Speaks to Her Daughter

Only one hour.

A nurse
tucked you up
placed you in my shaking arms

so I could lean in
smell you:
nothing newer on this planet
your eyes
met mine
and that is all we had.

For the first week
when I heard a baby cry
my breasts leaked, then
they stopped
and somehow my body
returned, left only
stretch marks, cartography of you.

From My Brother's Birth Mother

List of policies:

There will be no eye contact allowed between you and your baby.
There will be no breastfeeding.
There will be no opportunity for you to change your mind.

You cannot possibly give your child the best.

You will be sedated.
You will not hold your baby.
You cannot name your baby.

I was not a true mother.

crimes against the birth mother:

no alternatives presented,
no supports or financial assistance
offered, hiding the baby from the mother (including
transporting the baby to another location),
not informing the mother
they could legally reclaim
the baby before an adoption
order was signed.

from Civil Rights Crimes in Adoption, Dian Wellfare "in their rapacious quest for newborns the adoption industry forgot the law"

From My Birth Mom to Me

Let's be clear right off the bat;
I don't want to know anything
about you. It's high time
you gave up this romantic idea of finding me.
I don't want to be found, in fact.

You think you need to find your roots,
some kind of history, medical,
or that genealogical stuff?
It's all the rage now, isn't it, ancestry.com?
You think you need to know what happened
almost sixty years ago, between
a man, a woman?
That's none of your business, that.
Think you need family?
What, like half-siblings who won't think
you've popped up from under a rock,
complicating their lives?
Or me, some kind of warm embrace.
Just forget it, all of it.

Give up.
Leave me alone.
I am not waiting for you.

And your biological father; why
not worry about that half?
In fact, you should worry
about him. He was a bad one:
you're probably a bad seed.
That's why we aren't family, we don't have
criminals in our line.

record likely destroyed

missing pieces

• this is a personal matter and I don't want
my daughter to contact me
• I never want to hear from her
• veto

Veto

stone in my palm
I ask
what am I for

I am a Cupboard. Maybe.

"the past is buried in you, it's turned your flesh into its own cupboard"
—Claudia Rankine, *Citizen*

If what I am
is a cupboard, containing, if
I contain in my flesh
abandonment, what then
of the cellular joinings
beneath my bones,
my desolate wood shelves?

Doors
jammed shut.
Handles missing.

Driving East

Empty roads and long reach of sky, flickers of fence posts, ditches
filled with water, sedges, high cattails.   We've driven hours

prairie sprawls. A red-winged blackbird commands attention. Dust
seeps through the car.

My husband next to me, our exchanges unfold in pauses, radio
a tinny distraction, background mumble with road tread hum.

Suddenly, her angry voice (unprovable but I take as gospel)
on a radio program

My daughter can never come looking for me. I don't want
to know her, see her. She should leave me alone.

I am certain.
She has buried me.

I pull off, the ditch too close,
the car tilts

and I cry
untethered as prairie storm clouds

hollow as the wind's circling palm.
The sky presses heavier than earth.

Silences

Silence looks like fog
in hill hollows, smells like
the curled shell on the beach

endures the way a bird
bush-balanced, feather-shivered, becomes
a trembling note.

Listen, sit
in stillness:
this is the time to stop, let nothing distract.

This
then, is the hum
of silence.

When My Brother Found His Birth Mom

Her hungry mouth at his ear promised
a velvet cloak
a talking fox
and a castle

but when he visits,
the mortar has crumbled
the walls fall in and she sits
on a lumpy couch.

When My Sister Found Her Birth Mom

I don't want to find any old story.
I don't want to find a woman

in a cheap apartment, TV blaring,
half-sister on the couch beside her.

I don't want a man, guilty as charged, imprisoned,
to share my genes.

I don't want the anger or dysfunction
or the ugly bruising of lies.

I want her biological family:
the mother with high cheekbones mirroring hers

four instant brothers,
adoring, accepting.

I stand back, watch her story
unfold.

One Story of How

In telling my brother's story of search and find to a friend
I stumble into my sister's story:
opened my mouth and
a memory I didn't know I owned
fell out
(a memory I am not even sure was true)
fell into the lap of this friend
who picked it up, turned it in her hand twice,
recognized the name, family friends,
which became a dance of compare and check
(her cousin who recalled the adoption paper)
and we danced with dates and times and names
until I knew I had found my sister's birth mom
in a complete coincidence.
All that was needed was their permission.
Agreed and that was that.

And then it was theirs.

Memory Breakage

Memory breaks surface, sinks.
Currents run their course, a rip
of colliding tides and
I am tossed.

I want to refute
bruises on an arm, doors
slammed, pounding fists.
Perhaps

I didn't, but I wanted to.
You are wrong
about me. Perhaps
I am a liar.

One more blossom
drops, discoloured
along its edges.

Lois Speaks after Meeting Her Daughter's Birth Mother

How could I not come and meet
the woman who birthed my second?

I came to thank her.

I came to watch my daughter stand
next to her, see who she leaned towards.

I came with fear,
to protect my daughter, our family.

I wore blue.

I was blue.

I said, "It's a good thing your dad
isn't here, it would've hurt him."

I drank tea and looked at this woman, soft-spoken
who birthed my daughter.

I know I said thank you
as the floor felt tilted and I felt I was losing,

felt the sudden shift.
She would have been a fine mother.

Threads

I tug at a thread,
wind it up,
find the frayed end.

In my box of embroidery skeins,
I've sorted colours, untangled them,
brought order to their being.

I can darn a hole in a sock, rejoin what
has come undone; weave
in a running stitch back-and-forth

but it's never a complete fix: colour not
a perfect match, stitches never
lie as flat as I'd like, the wool a little askew.

Wild Goose

I have
applied to the government adoption registry
combed through phone books and cold-called
tracked obituaries
researched teachers in Ontario in 1958
looked at marriage registries
searched newspaper archives, taken
a genealogy test, but
can't find

what I have, so sparse,
dark grey feather
on water's surface.

Collected Data

I was listed as Baby Girl Walkom

Last name could be the father's. Or mother's.

Mother's date of birth? No
Father's date of birth? No
Medical Information? No

Non-identifying Information
They were both 23.
She was a teacher.
He was moon-faced.

There was a probationary year, in case I was defective.
My mom and dad applied for a male infant.
Let me tell you what I could pretend:

Pretense

When I was six
I wanted a tambourine
a caravan and a pied pony.
Pictures of me then, in
my mother's blue swirling skirt,
brass curtain hoops looped
over my ears for earrings, paisley
headscarf tied,
the story of me, gypsy, stolen from.

When She Learned Her Father Was the Moon

she climbed the tallest tree in the backyard
and waited for him to appear
over the neighbour's fence, but he arrived, tucked up
and curled, a half-moon with unformed features.

When she learned the moon was her father, she rented
a boat, rowed to the horizon to welcome him. But
he stalled behind clouds, blurred and distant: lit
only a fraction of her face.

The moon is her father, a word.
Her father is a word, distant.

There are weeks when she forgets
to watch for him, and he'll surprise her:
caught in tree branches, framed
by rooftops, reflected in a lake.

Blood moon rising.

Notes He May Have Written

1. June 15, 1960

It was her fault.
I never knew.
I have no genetic problems.
It was one night.
No doesn't always mean—
I was drunk, I was young
and her skirt was short.

2. August 21, 1960

It was all about her.
I was just the asshole that got her there.
She was the one that was on the line, how
heads turn and folks talk.
I drove her to Alberta before that could happen.
She wasn't going to teach that September.
She never spoke the whole way.
You call that passive aggressive nowadays.
I dropped her at the unwed mothers' home.
She didn't even want me to come in, to interview
with the agency. I drove her all that way
and she didn't even say thank you.

3. January 4, 1998

You have her eyes.

I wonder
where you got that temper?

I have always
wanted a daughter like you.

Wonder what her life is like, where
she settled.

You wouldn't know,
would you?

Severed

When you finally receive the file
lines blacken the papers
black slashed through your birth mother's age
her birthplace
a reason for the choices, to
family genetics
no history, no thread to tie it together.

Instead,
words, blocked, heavy, obsidian.

So you write the forms out in your own hand
and for every black stroke across the page
fill in what could have been,
write a story that just could be true.

The Story That Could Be

Dear Baby Jane Walkom,
I give you this name, my mother's middle one, and because you were born in January, so it seems fitting. you will get this letter if your adoptive parents give it to you,
or if you decide to apply for information from the Alberta adoption registry.
When you do, I want you to have answers.

Please know that I loved you as soon as I knew I was pregnant. Perhaps you wonder why did I give you up for adoption?

Because I loved you so much, but I didn't love your father.
He wasn't the man I thought he was, he was too young to be a father. Charming, smart, but I will always think of you.

Cold Calling

I am hot and
my hands tremble when dialing.
I ask for a Walkom,
(the woman that may be----)

There's a male voice on the other end.
There's no answer.
I have called so many numbers,
grasping at any possible----

How can I even ask the right questions?
I don't know your first name
ask for any female Walkom
listen for hesitations, a clue.

Perhaps you
are listening
from the hallway, whispering
tell her to go away.

No One Looks for the Father

He was married, worked at the same company,
sure, she can give you his name, but
no one searches for the father.

He was the farm hand, worked with her father and she fell
for him hard, his dark side, depression;
no one searches for more on their father.

He was 23 years old and there is no more to follow.

The Veil

When I wear it
I am field
wrapped in snow
that shrouds my geography.

When I wear it
I am lake
with early morning mist
rising in clouds of bafflement.

I hold the veil
frayed and threadbare,
pin it to my cheeks.
And I am hidden.

III

Could One of These Stories Be Mine?

Case Studies

Part 1 **Did You Hear?**

Did you hear the one about the young woman
who was nineteen when she learned she was adopted?
She left the house and never returned.

Did you hear about the woman
who taught her birth son in grade three and
never told a soul?

Did you hear about the man who, after he met
his birth mom living in poverty,
put on thirty pounds?

How she told her girlfriends, she was adopted, and chosen.
Specially.
They wanted to be chosen too.

Did your brother tease that you were adopted, and now, a moment
on a bed beside your mother and she asks you, isn't it strange you're
the only one with green eyes?

Did you hear about the family who sent
their adoptive son back after twelve years into foster care?
He'd "stolen" a piece of cake.

Did you hear that he doesn't want to know his background,
but his adoptive mom knows his father is German, and he's been
living in Germany for years, says it feels like home.

Part 2 Borderland

If I told you I needed
to know, I'd be lying.
I don't mind empty
pockets.
I didn't need
their names, maybe
medical markers, maybe
baseline for cancer or depression,
just write it out
and mail to me.

But they came looking for me,
walked in through
the gene door
asked I call
them mother and father,
built this strange
borderland where
we meet.

Part 3 **Adoption Now**

And what of adoption now?
: no choice
: no longer matched
by similar physical characteristics
or educational backgrounds

: fewer children

: their needs greater

: placed in prospective adoptive families later

A family takes in a bundle
of shredded emotions
and implodes on their love
of a small broken being

Part 4 Rapid Adoption

Months of rubbing my growing belly and then your flutterings go still. Not a smidge of fear until the next midwife visit and her wooden Pinard horn shakes. Then it's tender hands, ultrasounds, and the Consult: you are coming sooner, no help for it, laid in my arms for goodbye. I should have said a thousand other goodbyes to you. Then we're told there's a baby waiting to take your place, a baby no one seems to want and along comes your understudy. Snugged in flannel, wet and red-blotched. A nurse positions my arms and we're told "He's yours if you want him."

Dian Wellfare article, 1967 Adoption Act Australia ruled; parents of a recently stillborn child, not having intended to adopt, were offered a substitute baby to replace their dead infant. It was considered ideal if the mother could go home with the baby from the hospital, thus easing breastfeeding.

Part 5 Rapid Loss

He would be twenty now
I was told he was gone
stillbirth
taken for adoption instead

Part 6

Is She or Isn't She One of Us?	Is He or Isn't He One of Us?
I hear your questions.	I hear your questions.
Where to find her? Maybe	Where to find him? Maybe
at the edge of family photos	at the edge of family photos
perched on the arm of the couch,	perched on the arm of the couch,
near the back	near the back
maybe she was away that day.	maybe he was away that day.
questions, more questions:	questions, more questions:
is she really your child?	is he really your child?
But her hair:	But his hair:
How —	How —
they never finish the sentence.	they never finish the sentence.
I hear your questions	I hear your questions

We hear
How can—

is she really is she your child?	is he really is he your child?

Part 7 Dresser Drawers

It's usually the top one, filled with the rolled sock pairs, medley
of pins, stamps, scarves, broken costume jewelry, wallets no longer used
perhaps the passport, nylons, scents of powder in compacts.

Clear up her worldly goods. Find a tender secret.
In the back of her drawer; a flowered card, a photo.

Or adoption papers. A mother's name, so beautiful, so foreign.

Or discover your wife never told you about her move to Toronto
when she gave up her baby.

Or find you have an older sister, born in a separate province, born
years before you, unnamed, never spoken of.

Slide the drawer closed as your throat closes
on the fist-sized weight.

The Foundling's Story

Westerlies blew her here
along with thunderclouds and hail.
Of her origin, that's all I know.
She came in dark wet cold.
I opened the door, let her in.

What is first only the night, is then a day, a week.
Then tasks are given, regular, and I'd see
her on the stairs, carrying. In the kitchen too.
I laid outside her door late
nights, heard sobbing.

Followed her to barns
and river, watched her learn
local routes and lilt until
her voice sounded
sometime belonging.

Most let their questions drop.
I held mine close for all our sakes.
When westerlies returned would
she leave with them?
When the year was out, I realized not.

Who should wear the name and
who should be allowed? Here's
what I would do: hold a mirror to her face
on a full moon, watch her float, ask
for spun straw, place peas beneath her mattress.

I will ask her three
questions, find where she aims.

The Changling's Story

I won't see family ever again, I won't.
If you ask, I only have a sister
in Lincoln, doesn't travel. I have
no brother.

In a family photo, us three: brother
two sisters on church steps, of Sunday dressed,
hold it, see those well shined shoes and handed down clothes:
I tell you isn't any of my kin, it is clean forgot, cleaned-up.

I walk out into a new neighborhood and don't:
I don't sing. Those old songs gone.
Funny how one drop, one small drop will make.
Speak of blood, bloodlines and no brother, ever.

If they ask me.
What are you?
Sailing
away into whiteness.

Pearl's Typed Letters

To type love on the page
was all she wanted,
keys to tap dance
but at the speed of yearning, keys
jammed, type bars snarled and
her fingers purpled with blurred ink.

Some days the carriage arm that clasped
the page loosened.
Some days, hearts could move
when shift keys were depressed.
Her own heart ribboned over the pages
assailed by the *fflury* of keys.

Is attachment a portable device?
She removed and inverted the ribbon, more
blue ink on her hands from this 1962 Alpina
that heaved words at the page
the letters, the file cards, the smudged words
written for her son.

Naming

(When Keeping the Baby)

Your eyes widen to light after all that dark pressing
and I look deep too, find your colour,
the blue of ocean fathoms.
Your toes spread to new air.
The crease at the back of your neck
is the path to my heart.
I touch those miniscule fingernails,
chitin, the same protein
in the scales of a butterfly's wing.
You are morpho blue,
you are water and flight.

We must hold all this close to name you.

Naming

(When Relinquishing the Baby)

I gave you Lucy.
They took it.

I named you Jack.
That name was stolen from you.

I called you Corrie after my grandmother.
I don't know your name now.

Baby Girl
will do fine.

Your name is Matt.
In my heart.

I will always think of you
as Gwen.

Shame is a Tattoo on Their Shoulders

1.
Not sure how I got pregnant.
Didn't know about giving birth.
Labour was a shock. I cried
for help, no food, no nurses,
completely alone.

2.
My boyfriend cared about me,
wanted to visit
but at the door of the Beulah
they turned him away,
said I wasn't there.

3.
We were selfish
if we mentioned
that we wanted
to keep
our babies.

4.
Never told my mother I was pregnant.
I went off, was going to try work
in Saskatchewan. I sent a little money
back each week to prove it.
Don't know if she guessed.

5.
My mother brought me home in silence
from the unwed mother's home in Edmonton.
We drove hours without speaking.
She took me to my room, and told me,
"You won't speak of this ever again."

6.
I had three weeks with my baby.
They wouldn't let us breastfeed.
But still,
I held and bathed and bottle fed
her. One day, she was gone.

IV

As It Is Now

Testing, Testing, One Two Three

1.
The DNA kit arrives in the mail.
My daughter, who works in a vet clinic says
there's a similar service for dogs.
You send in a picture of the dog though.

2.
My husband takes a few pictures as I spit
into the clear plastic vial.
I am doing something,
finally, I will have an answer.

3.
The testing site offers
to build my family tree.
I type in the only name I have.
And find nothing further.

4.
There is a pie chart,
a link to the web site.
68% Scottish/English/Welsh
14% western European
8% Irish
4% Scandinavian 2% Finnish. For some reason, they are separate.
2% Jewish and 2% West Asian

5.
I am fractions.
I want story.

Root Bound

Upheaval as tree roots split
the concrete sidewalk,
searching nutrients.
Finally, new metaphor for search.
Fifteen feet from the tree,
my shovel bares
a maze of roots, with
tiny saplings angling for sun,
begging for any light on the matter.
Roots twist, cinnamon brown and sly,
innocent as they spread.

When tilling roots,
slow, go further down. Listen
for pre-lingual signals.
Cells intuit
more than written history.
Take loam, rock.
Peat and bone. Take
the mycorrhizal web, multitudes of insects
and blood and history, counting back.

I write the letter, begin Dear Family.
I write to ask which language
I would have worn,
for my tongue is wanting.
Whose eyes? Whose temper?
Whose sadness stains my capillaries and genes?
My roots were entwined in bedrock until
I was torn from shorn off.
They never knew of me
and so I am as if dead.

(based on Job 18)

Promise Made:

I am done
hauling uncertainty. Instead

I will carry wind
on my back.

Carry sheerness of rain,
the cloak of it.

Carry a pleated new moon
in my fist

its weight captive
and compressed.

I name these elements,
and I will wear them.

Perhaps
they are kin.

After Being Asked to Name My Ancestors in the Circle to Acknowledge the Territory We Visit

What do I wear of my father's blood?
What do I wear of my mother's?
I beg my ancestors to step forward,
reveal the stories beneath my skin
for the genes I carry are circuits of
surprise, those children I've borne
without my features, blue-eyed,
hair resolutely straight.

Can you deny that the first day
we look at our newborn
we are searching for traces?
The shorthand for
she is like her grandmother.

I can't unpack boxes
that will spill secrets I need,
can only feel the chorus of platelets
gathering at the site of injury.

The Places that Claim Me

"certain geographies feel like home—not by story or blood but merely by their forms and colours… how there are 'places that claim you… how you can fall in love with the light.'"
—Ellen Meloy, *The Anthropology of Turquoise*

The Bow River knows my name.
Spring runoff, snow melt.
Look how the sandbar is below water now.
Elk step cautiously into the current near a snarl
of twisted branches, logs. Walk the bank.

I belong in this temperate rainforest, the moss, the fine licorice
scented ferns,

or the boreal, scrubby, trembling aspen, spruce
lean and wind tilted.

I belong in a forest, its lines
reminding me to slow, hear my foot-falls.

When lake swimming, there is only skin.
Only water
Only skin
Only water
Only skin

The land will not lie.
If it wants you, it will burst with owning.
Place your hands here, fall to the ground/

Losses Add Up

The house when they raised it on skids. A pair of gloves.
My best friend when I stole an English shilling.
Another best friend when I sulked.

That summer no one watered
the garden; spinach bolted,
only one zucchini survived.

The cabin at Spruce Lake and the field
where silver-haired crocuses bloomed.
A forest was felled. A marsh drained.

All those boxes from the last move
sent to Value Village.
Unopened. Long gone.

Tell me everything—
it will go in the report:
passport, money, and bank cards,
soft denim shirt and sunglasses, make-up,
the key chain from my nephew, the camera
and some very expensive hair styling gel.

Tell me everything you lost:
I lost a father, a mother and family, then,
I lost a father and mother again.

Fragments

The first time we made a mosaic,
we built a gazebo in our backyard.
Everything was scavenged. We used
chipped tiles in odd colours, crafted
the floor mosaic as a lavish bouquet.

For the next, at our front stairs, golden carp
curved in dark blue water. And this summer,
on the concrete you poured, our daughter drew
leaning sunflowers, our grandson smashed tiles
the way a three-year-old was meant to.

I know only four people on earth
who hold me in their bones:
two children, two grandchildren,
my fragments of red, blue, green,
fashioning my small world.
Barely a flower, barely a leaf.

Nomad

Home is tucked and carried.
It is the welcoming stone in the valley.
The one to pick up, slip in a pocket.
Home is folded, then unfolded.
It is the pause after longing for movement.

Home changes colour with each horizon.
Speak the direction travelled out-loud.
Let home be a touch on the back of a hand.
Let it be the skin of the shadow you lie beneath.

Home is water, solace and dirt roads.
Home is a mirage, a standing pool of water.
It is the yellow dog beneath the tree, who follows you.
And the spirits, who would follow you too.

Home is collapsible. It is a four-letter word, a canyon,
a container for sad desires, small satchels of loss.
It is a wavering line you cannot lean
against; it shifts then disappears.

Speculative Fiction

In another world,
I am still your child.

We accept each other's
semblance:

when we speak
soft in anger

and a tendency
to hoard books and scarves.

We share language codes.
Follow familial lines of migration.

You've woven chants
through my hair since babyhood

and lines of salt current
hold us close.

You say
our eyes match.

Last night, an orange moon. Dogs howl

and I wake early. This morning's sun is red.

Mountains across the strait hide
like a rope line from the bow, submerged.

Deer sleep in my neighbour's yard, leave
comma shapes pressed in sunburnt grass.

I walk down the hill through crows' scorching
scolds. So much smoke haze in the sky.

I'll sit on the porch this evening,
let the ashes fall in my lap and

sip gin though it gives me grief, watching
as shadows flinch past the fence.

[**Insert**]

the poem I write
when I find
blood
relations

The Child Only Wants to Know

"Each tiny piece of new background material adds to personhood"
—from *The Stranger Who Bore Me*

I don't know the colour
of your eyes, the books you read, the worries
of your days, but wear your burdensome shadow.

I don't know the line of horizon
you long for, or the one smell from your childhood
you'd want at your death.

I don't know the words you say
to comfort, the poem you've memorized.
I don't know your hands.

Tell me. Start
with my growth in your womb, your
fears, your hunger for my leaving.

Tell me our family's ways: was land their faith?
Were they miners, bookish, dark, ordinary folk?
Did they vision and build? Did our family tear down?

What lullabies sung to the babies, food
cooked for the sick, for celebrations? What
offerings made? What words for anger?

Give me more than false
imaginings, empty medical records
and broken lineage.

It is story I want.

I am a child of

I come from

V Appendix

This Changes Everything.
This Changes Nothing.

Ice

You can't breathe below the ice.

Cold owns you. Trout mock your flail.

Skin splits: ice shards in the water are razors.

Ice and cold and breath and shards conspire.

If there is a way out, it is farther upriver

where your body crash-landed.

You have no breath, and so

you have no words—

there is no way to call.

In Conception Park

His eyes, like some scarred candle
at an altar blazed
and burnt her body

his greening breath
a clutch of thorns
latched onto skin

a dark unknown being
crouched
to feed

to carve her flesh:
and cast her
on this wretched path

In 1997, I wrote the night of my conception
as a rape poem, little knowing it to be true.

Take Back Your Secret

It won't be night's bitter air, but the snow
on a winter's afternoon
falling, soft, building a new landscape.

Perhaps there's a path where you wait,
hold a token, or let it hide in your pocket.
Keep it.

There is an empty bowl and
an unmarked envelope. Set them down,
let the secret be the missing, the dislocated.

There are no tracks in the snow.
Perhaps you're the scoop of a wing or
the moon beneath my tongue.

Acknowledgements

Many thanks to my first (and sometimes second and third) readers. I am beyond grateful that you are in my life as writers and friends. Your careful attention to this work and your probing questions have encouraged me to go further, deeper and harder. Thanks to Arleen Paré, Isa Milman, Barbara Herringer, Terry Ann Carter, Sue Gee, Barbara Black, Nancy Yakimosi, Wanda Hurren and Julia Ready, and then to Betsy Warland, and Anita Lahey.

And to those who shared their stories of adoption: thank you from the bottom of my heart for your trust and open-heartedness. Thank you to Pearl, Karen, Kristina, Shannon, Liz, Morva, Helene, Jennifer, Jon, Julius and Brooke, and those who wished to remain anonymous.

To Vici and Caitlin Press for giving this a home.

PHOTO: NANCY YAKIMOSKI

About the Author

Beth Kope grew up in Alberta and is honoured to live, work, and play in Victoria, BC, Coast Salish territory of Lekwungen and W̱SÁNEĆ nations. She has published two poetry collections. *Falling Season* (Leaf Press, 2010) detailed her mother's decline due to an aggressive form of dementia called Lewy Body. Her second book, *Average Height of Flight* (Caitlin Press, 2015), was a meditation on West Coast landscape and grief. Her work has also been included in three anthologies: *Refugium: Poems for the Pacific* (Caitlin Press, 2017), *Sweet Water: Poems for the Watersheds* (Caitlin Press, 2020) and *Voicing Suicide* (Ekstasis Editions, 2020). She is the co-host, along with Yvonne Blomer, of the annual Forest Poet-Tree event which is part of the Victoria Festival of Authors.